Understanding

CW00538004

FEEDING
YOUR BABY

Elizabeth Fenwick

Published by Family Doctor Publications Limited
in association with the British Medical Association

IMPORTANT

This book is intended to supplement the advice given to you by your doctor. The authors and publisher have taken every care in its preparation. In particular, information about drugs and dosages has been thoroughly checked. However, before taking any medication you are strongly advised to read the product information sheet accompanying it. Your pharmacist will be able to help you with anything you do not understand.

© Family Doctor Publications 1996

Medical Editor: Dr Tony Smith
Consultant Editor: Jane Sugarman
Cover Artist: Colette Blanchard
Medical Artist: Angela Christie
Design: MPG Design, Godalming
Printing: Reflex Litho, Thetford, Norfolk, using acid-free paper

ISBN: 1 898205 34 5

Contents

A tiny drop of Infacol

Can make a difference in a little life

When your baby is fed, warm and dry, it should be time for restful sleep.

But if baby is crying in pain, and you can't tell why, colic might be the cause.

Don't worry, just one or two droppers full of Infacol taken before every feed can bring relief, and make such a difference to baby's life and yours.

CONTAINS SIMETHICONE

Clinically proven to relieve infant colic and griping pain.   Always read the label.

The first decision – breast or bottle?

INTRODUCTION

Everything we know about the relationship between diet and health shows us that how children are fed as infants and toddlers matters. We know that what children of this age eat not only affects their normal growth and development, but also influences their health as adults.

This booklet describes what babies and toddlers need throughout this crucial stage in their lives, and how you can influence their eating habits so that they grow up enjoying the kind of diet that will keep them healthy. You'll find that it isn't difficult, it isn't even expensive, to feed your baby in a way that will lay strong foundations for a healthy future.

One of the first decisions you and your partner will have to make is whether your baby should be breast-fed or bottle-fed. You may even have made it before your baby was born, and probably you were influenced by what your mother or your friends have told you about breast-feeding and how your partner feels about it. But if you are thinking only of what is best for your baby, there is only one decision you can make. Breast-

feeding gets a baby off to a flying start. There is no better food for a baby than breast milk.

If you are undecided, it may help to look at some of the pros and cons.

WHY BREAST-FEED?

- Breast milk is a complete food – the ideal food for every baby. It can't 'disagree' with the baby; it is easy to digest and has exactly the right blend of nutrients for a newborn baby. What is more, its composition changes constantly to meet the baby's changing needs. Even formula milks which have been specially prepared for newborn babies are not as good. Breast milk contains special fats (called long chain polyunsaturated fatty acids or LCPs) which are thought to be important for brain development in the first three months of life.
- Breast milk contains antibodies which help protect the baby from disease, until his own antibody-forming system has matured. Formula milk can't provide this protection.
- If there is allergy in your family, breast-feeding will protect your baby.
- Breast milk is always sterile, and always at the right temperature. Bottle-feeding involves expense, equipment, sterilisation and time.
- Breast-fed babies are rarely overweight – it is easier to overfeed a bottle-fed baby.
- Breast-feeding may give more pleasure to the baby. Babies like to suck. Sucking is a need and a pleasure quite distinct from the need for food. Breast-feeds tend to last longer than bottle-feeds: when a bottle is finished, the mother removes it and the feed is over. There is no such obvious end-point to a breast-

Breast-feeding straight after birth

feed; it is usually the baby who decides when the feed has gone on long enough. And this will probably be when he has had enough sucking, as well as enough milk.

- Because of the baby's need to suck, in the early weeks a brief breast-feed is usually the easiest way to soothe a crying baby.
- Once you are used to it, breast-feeding is in many ways easier and more convenient for you. No special equipment or sterilisation is involved. If you are travelling with your baby, going on holiday or simply going out for the day, breast-feeding is much simpler.
- Most women who breast-feed get enormous pleasure from it, and love the feeling of intimacy it creates between them and their babies.

WHY BOTTLE-FEED?

- Bottle-feeding makes it easier for someone else to care for your baby during the day, if you have to go out or go to work.
- Your partner can take turns at feeding, so that you can have an occasional good night's sleep. Being involved in feeding gives your partner a chance to build up his relationship with the baby too.
- The baby may cry less, need feeding less often in the early weeks than a breast-fed baby.
- You need never worry that the baby isn't getting enough milk, because you can see exactly how much is taken.
- Tiredness, illness or stress, which can all temporarily reduce your breast milk, won't affect the bottle-fed baby's feeds.

Fathers can feed baby with a bottle

It is worth remembering that, if you start to breast-feed and it does not seem to work for you, you can always stop. And even if you breast-feed only for a few days, you will be providing your baby with valuable antibodies which will help fight infection in this newborn period. But once you have started bottle-feeding, you can't change over to breast-feeding, because without the stimulation of your baby sucking, your breasts will stop producing milk.

However, it's important to choose the way that feels right for you. Feeds should be enjoyable for both you and your baby. If you breast-feed only because you think you ought to, or if you bottle-feed but feel uncomfortable about doing it, feeds won't be a source of pleasure. However you feed your baby, the closeness and contact between you are as important as the nourishment you are giving. You can breast-feed successfully even if you have small breasts. The size of the breast is determined by the amount of fatty tissue, not the number of milk-producing glands, which is more or less the same whatever the size of the breast.

Your breasts may be slightly smaller after weaning, because some of the fatty tissue has been replaced by milk glands, but you will probably regain your pre-pregnancy figure more quickly if you breast-feed, because the fat

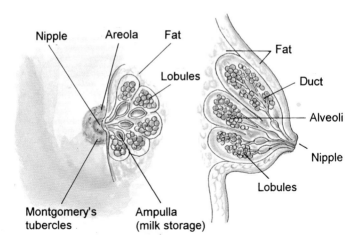

Increase in milk-producing glands makes the breasts larger and heavier

reserves laid down in pregnancy are drawn upon for milk production. Breast-feeding stimulates uterine contractions too, and helps the uterus to return to normal. Even if you are ill, your illness won't affect the baby. However, if you have a general anaesthetic for any reason, you won't be able to feed the baby for a few hours afterwards, because the drugs will pass into your milk.

You will know when your baby is hungry because he will tell you – by crying. Hunger isn't the only reason a baby cries but in the early weeks it is the most usual one. If feeding and cuddling soothes him only for a short time, and if he cries most at one particular time of day, usually during the early evening, he may have 'three-month colic'. this usually starts when the baby is about three weeks, and is a harmless and common condition – it is not real 'indigestion' and is nothing to do with the way you are feeding your baby. It is distressing for you because there is so little you can do to comfort your baby, but you can be assured that by about three months it will have disappeared.

KEY POINTS

✓ What we feed our infants and toddlers affects them in later life

✓ The first decision about feeding is whether to breast-feed or bottle-feed

✓ Breast-feeding gets your baby off to the best possible start

✓ Nearly every woman can breast-feed successfully if she is given the right advice

Breast-feeding your baby

Breast-feeding is easy – if you are given the right help to begin with. When breast-feeding fails it is nearly always either because the woman doesn't really want to do it, or because no-one has explained to her how to make breast-feeding work.

However, it sometimes takes a while for a baby to get the hang of breast-feeding, and for the milk supply to become established. If you were half-hearted about starting in the first place, it's easy to become discouraged in the early days, and convince yourself that it's just not going to work for you. If the decision to breast-feed was one you and your partner made together, his encouragement will make it much easier for you to go on.

MAKING BREAST-FEEDING WORK

These are the three simple rules which will help you establish successful breast-feeding:

1. Put your baby to the breast as soon as possible – immediately after birth if you can. Even if it is only for a short time, this early suckling seems to help breast-feeding later on.
2. Let your baby feed as often as he wants and take as much as he wants. Your breasts work on a supply and demand system. The more milk your baby takes, the more your breasts will make.
3. Resist the temptation to top your baby up with a bottle-feed because you think he is still hungry. If you satisfy his hunger this way he will take less from you, and your breasts will produce less milk than ever. Instead, breast-feed more frequently.

Demand feeding

Demand feeding simply means letting the baby feed whenever he is hungry and not according to a strict routine.

Most newborn babies need to be fed at least every three hours, and many demand food much more frequently than this at first. Breast-fed babies usually need more frequent feeds than bottle-fed babies, because breast milk is more easily and quickly digested than formula milk. Formula milk also contains more calories than breast milk, and delays feelings of hunger for longer.

There is nothing to be gained by keeping your baby waiting for a feed once he has woken up and is noisily demanding to be fed. He will only get so distressed that he refuses to suck until you have managed to comfort and calm him.

This rather chaotic period, when most of your day seems to be taken up just with feeding your baby, won't last long. As the baby's digestive system matures, he'll take more at each feed and the intervals between feeds will become longer. Gradually a more regular feeding routine will be established, although most breast-fed babies still need feeding every three hours until they are about one month old. Many don't settle down to a more-or-less four-hourly feeding routine until they are two to three months old.

How do the breasts make milk?
Whenever a baby feeds, a hormone, prolactin, is released into your

Prolactin released

Prolactin activates cells to secrete milk

Sucking stimulates nerve impulses

A hormone is released when your baby feeds which stimulates the milk-producing cells

bloodstream and stimulates the milk-producing cells so that they produce more milk. The more the baby feeds, the more milk is produced.

If you feel you have too little milk, you may be tempted to 'save it' rather than offer the baby frequent snacks, so that when the time comes for his 'real' feed you have plenty of milk. This is a mistake: if milk is left in the breast it tends to suppress the production of more milk. It's much better to let your baby empty your breast so that his sucking increases the amount of milk you produce. The less milk your baby takes from your breast, the less will be made. If you were to stop breast-feeding, your milk supply would soon cease altogether.

The let-down reflex
Another hormone, oxytocin, is also released into your bloodstream when your baby starts to feed. This makes the muscles around the milk-producing cells contract, so that milk is squeezed into the milk ducts ready for the baby to feed. It is this 'let-down' reflex which often makes one breast leak when the baby is put to the other. You can stop the flow by pressing your palm over the whole nipple area.

If you are very anxious or embarrassed about breast-feeding, the let-down reflex may not work

so well, so when you start a feed try to make sure that you are comfortable and relaxed and able to concentrate just on feeding your baby.

Foremilk and hindmilk
All the time you are breast-feeding the composition of breast milk changes according to your baby's needs. For the first few days after birth your breasts produce a creamy looking milk, high in protein, called colostrum. As well as all the nutrients your baby needs, it contains antibodies which pass your own resistance to some infections on to your baby. Even if you breast-feed for only a few days your baby will benefit from the colostrum.

After about three days your breasts start to produce milk. It looks more thin and watery than colostrum, but, again, it contains everything your baby needs. When you breast-feed, your baby doesn't need anything else. Even in hot weather the baby won't need extra fluid.

The first rush of milk the baby takes from your breast is a sweet, watery fluid called the foremilk, which is stored behind the areola. Its sweetness encourages your baby to suck, and the sucking stimulates the let-down of the main part of the feed – the hindmilk. This is richer and creamier than the foremilk and contains more calories and nutrients. A baby needs both foremilk and hindmilk. This is why it is better to let your baby feed steadily at one breast for at least ten to fifteen minutes at each feed, before changing over to the other breast. If you change breasts too soon, the baby will get a double dose of foremilk, but not enough hindmilk to satisfy his hunger. At the next feed, give the baby the other breast first.

GIVING A FEED

Babies are born knowing how to suck, with an instinctive reflex that makes them automatically 'root' for the breast. At first the baby may need a little help from you to find the nipple, and to latch onto it correctly.

It is important to make sure your baby feeds in the right position so that he can suck well and drain your breast efficiently. His head should be tilted back slightly, his chin pressed against your breast, and his mouth wide open so that he takes the whole areolar area inside. In this position your nipple will point towards the roof of his mouth, and his tongue and jaws will 'milk' the breast by pressure on the base of the areola (see page 11).

If feeding seems to be difficult for your baby or painful for you, it is almost certainly because the baby is not latched on to your breast in the right position. A baby who sucks only on the nipple won't get any milk – and will make your nipples sore.

Holding your baby

It's important to be comfortable and relaxed when you are feeding. Choose a low chair, sufficiently upright to support your back, and with no arms. Clothes that open

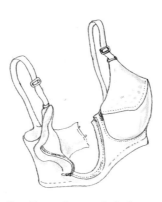

Bra with cups that open for feeding

down the front, and a front opening nursing bra, make feeding simpler, and allow your baby lots of 'skin contact'.

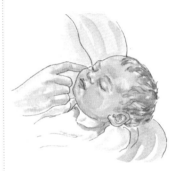

Stroke the baby's cheek to turn his head towards the nipple

- Hold your baby so that he lies on his side, facing you, his head slightly higher than his body. A pillow on your lap will raise the baby to a comfortable height for feeding. Make sure that your baby has a hand free to touch and stroke your breast.
- Bring the baby's head close to your breast. The baby's chin should touch the lower part of your breast. Touch the baby's upper lip with your nipple and, when his mouth opens, guide your breast into it, making sure he takes the whole areolar area into his mouth.

Baby supported by pillow to comfortable height

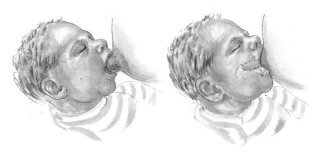

The right position of the baby on your breast

- If the baby doesn't seem to realise what is expected of him and turns his head away, stroke the cheek nearest to you with a finger, or with your nipple. This should make him turn his head towards your breast and open his mouth (don't try to turn his head towards you with your hand – this will just confuse him).

The right position

Once your baby is latched on to your nipple properly his jaws will be wide open so that his mouth is full of your breast. You will be able to see the muscles in his temples working as he sucks. But you shouldn't notice his cheeks going in and out – if they are, it means that he is not latched on in the right position.

Even if your baby's nose is tightly pressed against your breast there is no need to worry that he may not be able to breathe properly. Babies have snub noses which ensure that they can always breathe while they are feeding. There's no need for you to feel that you must press the breast down away from the baby's nose. In fact, if you do this you may pull the

Wind baby across the shoulder

breast away so that the baby cannot suck properly.

How long should a feed last?

Let your baby suck for as long as he wants so that he drains the breast. You can trust your baby to make it clear when he has had enough! He will let the nipple slip out of his mouth, turn his head away from the breast and obviously lose interest. Often a baby likes to pause in the middle of a feed, and then go back for a second helping. Sometimes he may simply go to sleep in the middle of a feed.

Take him off the breast and sit him up, or prop him against your shoulder to wind him. You can then offer your baby the other breast, in case he is still hungry.

A bottle-fed baby's feed usually has a natural end-point – the bottle is empty, so the mother removes it. A breast-fed baby's feeds tend to be longer, because he is more able to continue the 'comfort sucking' which most babies enjoy, even if the breast is almost empty.

If you feel the feed has gone on long enough, and your baby clearly does not want to let go, don't try to pull your nipple away while he is sucking – this will hurt! Either wait until he stops for breath, or slip a finger between your breast and his lips to break the suction.

Alternate the breast you give the baby first at each feed; the first

Use a clean finger to break baby's suction

breast usually gets the hungriest sucking and the most stimulation.

Sleepy babies

A newborn baby is often too sleepy to suck for long. Don't worry if your baby goes to sleep after a few sucks; don't try to wake him. He'll wake and feed again when he's hungry.

Feeding premature babies

A premature baby may take only a little milk at each feed, but will need very frequent feeds at first. However, these babies tend to sleep a lot at first, and don't always wake to demand the food they need. You may need to wake your baby every three hours and offer a feed.

Feeding twins

If you have twins and want to breast-feed, your breasts will be able to make enough milk. To begin with you will find it easier to feed them one at a time. Once you have

Feeding twins

all got the hang of breast-feeding, you should be able to feed both together. This is easiest sitting on a bed or sofa with plenty of cushions to support the babies. Experiment to find the most comfortable position – perhaps lying one baby across your lap in the normal way, tucking the legs of the other under your arm, or tucking both babies under your arms while cradling their heads in your hands.

Expressing milk

You can breast-feed and yet still leave your baby in someone else's care for a few hours, if you express breast milk to be given in a bottle. Most babies will accept this happily, though some refuse it with howls of indignation.

Many women find it easy to express by hand, others find a manual or electric pump is quicker and less tiring.

Before expressing, sterilise the equipment and wash your hands. The milk will flow more easily if you warm your breasts before you start.

Expressing by hand

Sit at a table with a sterilised bowl in front of you. First stimulate the flow of milk through the ducts. Support your breast in one hand and, with the other, massage the breast working downwards towards the areola, using your whole hand. Work your way all the way round the breast, including the underside. Massage all round the breast at least ten times.

Still supporting your breast in one hand, place your thumb half-

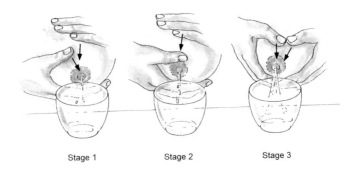

Stage 1   Stage 2   Stage 3

Expressing your milk

way up your breast and bring it down to the edge of the areola, pressing firmly all the time. Just behind the areola press firmly with your thumb and fingers, squeezing the areola up and in, 'milking' the

Suction draws milk from the breast

duct so that milk spurts out. After a few minutes repeat this process on the other breast; alternate the breasts until you have enough milk or until no more milk flows.

Expressing with a pump

The most efficient type of manual pump is in the form of a syringe, with an inner and outer cylinder. A funnel attached to the inner cylinder fits over the areola to form an airtight seal. As you draw the outer cylinder away from you the suction draws milk from your breast into it. The outer cylinder converts into a baby's bottle.

The electrical pumps which are used in hospitals are very efficient but much more expensive. You may, however, be able to hire one from a local National Childbirth Trust agent. Breast milk can be stored in a sealed bottle in the refrigerator for

24 hours, or it can be frozen and kept for up to two months in a freezer.

BREAST-FEEDING PROBLEMS

Most of the problems you are likely to have with breast-feeding will disappear once you and the baby have settled down and feeding is well established.

No-one is likely to force you to stop feeding if you want to continue, so don't be discouraged, and don't stop feeding; this will only mean that your breasts become engorged and make any problem worse.

Engorged or leaking breasts

When your baby is three or four days old you may wake up to find that your milk has 'come in' and your breasts are uncomfortably swollen and hard. If the areola is so swollen that your baby cannot easily latch on, express a little milk (see page 13); this will make you more comfortable and help your baby to suck properly.

At the start of a feed, when your breast is full, the milk may pour out so fast that it swamps her or makes her choke. You can reduce the flow by pressing gently upwards with a finger on either side of the areola, just beyond her mouth.

Your breasts may leak quite a lot until your milk supply settles down to match your baby's needs. Breast pads inside your bra will absorb the milk. Change them often: if your nipples are continually damp they may get sore.

SORE AND CRACKED NIPPLES

Sore nipples are sometimes a problem when you start to breast-feed, usually because the baby isn't latching onto the breast properly. Even lengthy feeds should not make your nipples sore if the baby is in the right position. It helps to dry nipples with warm air from a hair dryer after each feed, and let air get to them whenever possible.

If only one nipple is tender, rest it for 24 hours, expressing the milk, and feeding the baby from the other breast. You can give the expressed milk (which will keep in the refrigerator for 24 hours) from a bottle, too.

A shooting pain through your nipple as the baby sucks may mean that there is a tiny crack in your nipple. This will heal in a day or two, but meanwhile you should not feed the baby from that breast. You can express the milk (see page 13) and give it to your baby in a bottle or from a spoon.

Painful, lumpy breasts

A hard, tender lump in the breast means that one of the tiny milk ducts has become blocked. The solution is to let the baby clear it! Bathe the breast in hot water first, and massage it gently. Then put the baby to the breast. You may get a moment's intense pain as the baby starts to suck, but then the duct will clear and the pain and lumpiness will disappear.

Occasionally infection in a blocked milk duct causes mastitis. Part of your breast will be hard, red and throb painfully, and you may run a temperature and feel 'fluey'. Don't stop feeding from the infected breast, but do see your doctor that day. An antibiotic will probably be prescribed, because, if untreated, mastitis can lead to a breast abscess.

Breast milk jaundice

Mild jaundice is common in newborn and especially in pre-mature babies because their livers are not yet working efficiently. A very few newborn babies develop 'breast milk jaundice', for reasons which are not fully understood. However, it is not dangerous and need not stop you breast-feeding. Very rarely, a baby is so badly jaundiced that you may be advised to stop breast-feeding temporarily.

Breast-feeding and HIV

A mother who is HIV positive can transmit the infection to her baby in breast milk. The risk is small, but because it is avoidable, doctors recommend that women who are HIV positive or who have not been tested but know that they are in a high-risk group should not breast-feed their babies.

BABIES WHO GAIN WEIGHT SLOWLY

When you are breast-feeding you can't actually *see* what the baby takes, so it's natural sometimes to worry that he's not getting enough.

Babies do not all gain weight steadily or at the same rate. So don't worry if yours seems to be gaining less rapidly than other babies you know, or puts on less per week than the 'average' weight gain you see in growth charts. If your baby looks well and has frequent wet nappies (at least six in every 24 hours), he is almost certainly getting enough milk.

You need worry that your baby really is getting insufficient milk only if you notice that his nappy remains dry for more than six hours at a stretch or if he passes small amounts of dark green bowel motions instead of the normal soft, mustardy-yellow motions. A baby who is very dehydrated may be sleepy and listless too.

Sometimes a baby seems to be never off the nipple. He has very short but very frequent feeds, usually because his stomach is still too small to hold much milk. And yet he is fretful and puts on little weight. This may be because he feeds so briefly that he may be getting only foremilk. He won't be getting enough of the richer hindmilk because he doesn't suck for long enough. If you alternate the breast you offer first at each feed in the normal way, the next feed may be giving him only foremilk too. Too much sugary foremilk may give the baby frothy diarrhoea

If your baby seems to have this pattern of short, frequent feeds and is gaining little weight, try offering your baby the same breast at two or three successive feeds instead of alternating breasts each time. After about two hours do the same with the other breast, offering it each time and letting the baby suck for as long as he likes at each feed.

NIGHT FEEDS

A newborn baby makes no distinction between night and day. To begin with your baby may need to be fed as often during the night as during the day. Broken nights are part and parcel of life with a new baby – and unfortunately there is little you can do to alter this. Few babies are able to sleep more than five hours at a stretch without waking with hunger until they are at least six weeks old or weigh about 4.5 kg (10 lb). Until this age your baby will probably wake for a night feed as well as an early morning one at around 5.0 or 6.0 a.m.

Gradually though he will sleep for longer at a stretch during the night, and by the time he is three or four months old will probably sleep

Night feeds

for a five, six or even seven hour stretch at night, although he may feed just as often during the day. This lengthy period of sleep may not be when you want to be in bed and asleep yourself, however. Your baby may sleep well from, say, 7.0 p.m. to 1.0 or 2.0 a.m, then wake every two or three hours after this. Some parents try to encourage a more convenient pattern by waking their baby for a feed when they go to bed themselves, in the hope that he won't wake again. However, a baby who hasn't woken naturally through hunger probably won't eat much, and the chances are that he will simply wake up again a couple of hours later. It is probably easiest to let the baby settle into his own natural pattern. Meanwhile, he wakes because he is hungry, and there is nothing to be gained by letting him cry. The only solution is to feed him.

GROWTH SPURTS

The supply and demand system which makes breast-feeding work means that it will always be able to keep pace with the baby's growing needs.

However, as your baby grows, you'll find that every few weeks, just when you think he has settled into a less demanding feeding routine, your baby has a growth spurt and there will be two or three days when he seems to be hungry all the time. These growth spurts are usually around three weeks, six weeks, twelve weeks and six months. It usually takes about two days of frequent feeds to stimulate your breasts to make the extra milk the baby needs.

FEEDING YOURSELF

All *you* need to do to produce enough milk is to eat regularly, whenever you are hungry, drink whenever you are thirsty, rest as much as you can, and try not to get too tired. The baby's natural appetite will do the rest.

You will find you are much hungrier than usual while you are breast-feeding; it's quite normal to need as much as 800 calories a day more than usual. Some of these calories will come from the fat laid down during pregnancy, but you will need to eat more than usual too. Let your appetite guide you, but try not to have too long a gap between meals – even if you never usually eat breakfast, or have tended to skip lunch, you'll find you need three meals a day and snacks in between while you are breast-feeding. Don't try to diet while breast-feeding.

You can eat anything you normally eat while you are breast-feeding. In spite of the old wives' tales which abound, strawberries won't give your baby diarrhoea, garlic won't give him colic.

Breast-feeding won't prevent you getting pregnant. Even if you have not started your periods again you should use contraception. If you want to go on the Pill, talk to your doctor. The combined (oestrogen and progestogen) pill reduces your milk supply and shouldn't be taken if you are breast-feeding.

If you wait until your milk supply is well established, you should be able to take the mini-pill (progestogen only), though some women find they need to feed the baby more often when they first start to take it. Remember that if you have previously used a cap or diaphragm, you must have a new one fitted after the birth as the shape of your cervix will have changed.

WHEN SHOULD BREAST-FEEDING STOP?

This depends very much on how much you and your baby are enjoying it. As the baby starts to take more and more solid food, he will take less and less milk; the natural supply and demand system now works in reverse and the supply gradually tails off.

If you carry on breast-feeding till the baby is six months old you may be able to wean him straight onto a cup without having to introduce a bottle at all (see 'Weaning', page 38). But some babies do like a 'sucking' feed at bedtime until well into the second half of their first year. So if you don't want to continue this final breast-feed of the day, you may find your baby settles better if you give him a bottle instead.

GOING BACK TO WORK

Going back to work may be relatively easy if you live near enough to return home for feeds, or there is a crêche at work. If not, expressing your milk makes it perfectly possible for you to start work again and yet still continue to breast-feed.

- Get your baby used to taking an occasional bottle of expressed milk from somebody else well before returning to work.
- Stockpile expressed milk in your freezer for several weeks before you go back to work. It will keep for up to two months.
- Express milk during the day at work, to stimulate your milk supply. Store expressed milk in a fridge or insulated cool box with icepacks.

- Leave bottles of expressed milk for your baby's daytime feeds.
- If your milk supply needs boosting, give extra feeds during the evening and night.

KEY POINTS

✓ Breast-feed your baby on demand; this helps to stimulate milk production and ensure that the baby is not hungry

✓ Foremilk is the first milk produced by the breast but the second milk or hindmilk is the main part of the feed and is more nutritious

✓ Make sure that you are comfortable and relaxed when breast-feeding and that the baby is in the right position

✓ Breast milk can be stored frozen for up to two months

✓ You can get pregnant when breast-feeding

Bottle-feeding

Breast milk is the ideal food for a baby, but this doesn't mean that your baby will suffer if you do decide to bottle-feed. Provided you use the right kind of formula your baby will thrive. And there are some benefits in bottle-feeding too. First, your partner can take his turn at feeding the baby, and second, you know exactly how much milk your baby is taking.

When you are breast-feeding you are in such intimate contact with your baby that it is easy to hold him close and cuddle him against your skin, to look down into his eyes and smile and talk to him. All babies need this kind of loving attention, and it is just as important and just as easy to give it while you bottle-feed.

BOTTLE-FEEDING ON DEMAND

Just like breast-fed babies, bottle-fed babies should be fed whenever they are hungry. At first this may mean very frequent feeds, but at each feed the baby will only take what he needs. Newborn babies usually need as many as seven to eight feeds a day, and will take about two ounces at each feed. So long as you let the baby's own appetite guide you, there is no danger of overfeeding. In a few weeks the baby will settle down to a more regular pattern, needing a feed every three or four hours, and taking more at each feed. In fact, a bottle-fed baby usually needs to be fed less often than a breast-fed baby, because formula takes longer to digest than breast milk.

Right from the beginning, give your baby as much control over feeding as you can, so that the feed is something you enjoy together, not something that is 'done' to him. Let him set the pace, pausing to look around, play with the bottle or stroke your breast if he wants to.

Smile back at him as he takes time off to look up into your eyes, and talk or sing softly to him. Don't wrench the bottle away immediately it's empty, if the baby obviously still wants to go on sucking for a while. Above all, let him decide when he has had enough.

CHOOSING A FORMULA

Ordinary cows' milk isn't suitable for a baby until he is at least six months old. Until then, use a specially prepared infant formula. Infant formulas are artificial feeds, designed to be as similar to human breast milk as possible.

Most infant formulas are based on cows' milk. The main protein in the milk is either whey or casein (curds). Whey-based milks have been treated to make them more like breast milk and easier to digest, so they are most suitable for a young baby. Curd-based milks are less easy to digest. It is sometimes suggested that very hungry babies are more easily satisfied with a curd-based milk, and many mothers change from a whey-based milk to a curd-based milk as their babies grow older. There is no real evidence that this makes much difference. A better way to satisfy a hungry baby during the first three months is to offer feeds more frequently.

Vitamins and some minerals are added to infant formulas during manufacture, so that it contains everything the baby needs; you

need add nothing but water to it.

Very rarely, a baby is allergic to cows' milk. Breast-feeding is the ideal solution, but if this really isn't possible, your doctor or health visitor will probably suggest that you use a formula based on soya, a vegetable protein.

Some infant formulas are supplemented with a blend of fish oil which contains special fats (long chain polyunsaturated fatty acids, or LCPs). Many doctors believe that these fats, which are naturally present in breast milk, play an important part in the development of a baby's brain during the early weeks of life. For the first three months at least, it is worth spending extra money to buy this kind of formula, especially if your baby was born prematurely. Most formula milks don't contain these fats; Milupa is one manufacturer which does produce a milk (Aptamil) supplemented with LCPs.

Formula usually comes in the form of a powder, which has to be mixed with boiled water. Some brands of formula are also available as sealed cartons of ready-mixed formula. These are much more expensive, but very convenient if, for example, you are on a camping holiday. These milks have been ultra heat treated, and have a limited storage life. They must be stored in a cool place, and not used after the 'best before' date on the carton. Once opened, they can be stored in the fridge for up to 24 hours.

Once you have opened a packet of formula, keep it in the fridge. If your baby does not finish his bottle, throw the remains away – never keep it for the next feed.

MILK FOR THE OLDER BABY

Pasteurised milk is suitable for babies aged six months and over, and you can, if you wish, continue to give infant formula. But in both cases your baby will need to be given extra iron and vitamin D – ask your health visitor about this. 'Follow-up' milks – specifically prepared for older babies, with extra iron and vitamins added – are suitable too.

Once your baby is over a year, you should give whole cows' milk, which is a good source of energy, protein, calcium and vitamins. Breast milk and infant formula are no longer suitable (see also page 41).

THE NEED FOR GOOD HYGIENE

The main drawback of bottle-feeding is the need to protect your baby from bacteria that might cause stomach upsets or diarrhoea. Milk is an ideal breeding ground for these germs. So the bottles, and everything else that you use to make up the feed, must be sterilised every day, using a special sterilising solution. You can make up a whole day's supply of feeds at once, but because the germs multiply most easily at room temperature, the filled bottles must be put immediately into the fridge, and stored there until you need them (but for no longer than 24 hours). If you have no fridge, it is safest to make up each feed only when you need it.

Always wash your hands before preparing or giving a feed.

a. Wash thoroughly

THE EQUIPMENT YOU NEED

- Six to eight bottles (unbreakable and wide necked)
- Ten teats (either plain or moulded to the shape of a nipple)
- Funnel
- Measuring jug
- Long-handled spoon
- Sterilising bath
- Sterilising tablets
- Bottle brush
- Salt
- Knife

b. Sterilising tank

c. Use boiling water to rinse

STERILISING BOTTLES

Feeding equipment must be washed after use, and then sterilised

in a special purpose-built sterilising unit, or in any lidded plastic container. Most sterilising units hold only four to six bottles. So if you use one of these, for the first few weeks, when your baby may need at least eight feeds a day, you will need to sterilise bottles twice a day. But modern sterilising units are so quick and easy to use that this need not be too time consuming. Boil teats separately, or better still, use sterilising tablets – the teats will last longer.

Remember that the measuring jug, funnel, knife and spoon that you use should be sterilised too.

An electric steam steriliser is a quick, easy alternative way to sterilise equipment without the use of chemicals, but it will only take bottles and teats. Sterilisation takes under 10 minutes. The cost of a steam steriliser is about £30. Alternatively, feeding equipment can be sterilised in the old-fashioned way simply by boiling it for 25 minutes.

Domestic microwave ovens are not suitable for sterilising bottles. And although a dishwasher will wash bottles effectively, it will not sterilise them.

Sterilising routine

After each feed, throw away any milk left, rinse the bottle and teat in warm water, and set it aside until you have collected a batch for sterilisation.

Wash all the bottles and teats in warm soapy water. Use a bottle brush to remove all traces of milk. rub the inside of the teats with salt. Rinse bottles and teats thoroughly in cold water.

Fill the steriliser with ordinary cold tap water to the suggested level, and add the recommended number of sterilisation tablets.

Put the washed bottles and teats in the tank and leave for the recommended time. Make sure that they are fully submersed. Sterilisation is usually complete in about 30 minutes, but you can safely leave them in the tank until you are ready to make up the next batch of feeds. Rinse thoroughly with boiling water before use.

MAKING UP A FEED

Infant formula usually comes as a powder, to which you add boiled water. The instructions on the packet will tell you the right amount of formula and water to use when making up a feed, and the amount of feed your baby needs according to his weight and age.

Follow the instructions exactly when you are making up the feed, to make sure you get the proportions right. If you add too much formula, the feed may be dangerously concentrated, and the baby may gain too much weight. If you consistently add too little, your baby will be hungry and may gain weight too slowly.

The right kind of water

Until your baby is over six months, boil *all* the water you use to make up feeds – even if you are using bottled water. Babies over six

- Drain the sterilant from the steriliser and pour in boiling water to rinse the equipment. Wash your hands and take everything out, leaving it to drain on kitchen paper. Boil a fresh kettle of water to mix the feeds, and let it cool slightly (to about 70°C).

- Decide how many feeds you want to make up. If your baby is likely to want six feeds during the day, make up seven, so that you can put a little extra into each bottle. Pour the total amount of water that you will need into your sterilised measuring jug.

- Add the recommended number of scoops of powder. As you fill each scoop, level off the top with the back of a knife – be careful not to pack the powder down.

- When you have added the right number of scoops, stir the solution with a sterilised spoon until the powder dissolves.

- Pour the milk into sterilised bottles, adding a little more than the suggested amount, in case your baby is extra hungry at some feeds. You can make up a whole day's supply each morning.

- Put the teat, top first, into the bottle, and screw on the lid. The teat should not touch the milk; tip some out if necessary

- Put all the bottles straight into the fridge, and keep them there till they are needed.

months can be given ordinary tap water which needn't be boiled.

Always take water from the rising main (usually the cold water tap in the kitchen).

If you have a water softener, don't use softened water to make up feeds, but take all drinking water from the unsoftened supply. Softened water contains too much sodium to make it suitable for infant feeding. Boil water for feeds afresh each time.

Water which has been boiled repeatedly may also contain too much sodium. Water from private supplies isn't always suitable for infant feeding. If you use a private supply, it's best to ask your local authority whether the water is suitable for infants.

Old houses are sometimes plumbed with lead pipes, and sometimes this means that the tap water contains too much lead to make it suitable for making up

a. Use dry knife to level scoop

c. Pour the milk into sterilised bottles

b. Add scoops to boiled measured water

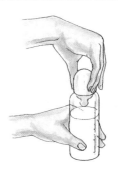

d. Put the teat, top first, into the bottle and screw on the lid

feeds. If your house has lead pipes, ask your local water authority to test your tap water. If it contains too much lead, you may be able to solve the problem simply by running off a basin full of water first, before you draw off the water to be used for feeds.

The first water to be drawn off will have been standing in the pipes for a while and is likely to contain more lead.

Bottled water

Bottled water is not sterile – until your baby is six months old it still needs to be boiled before being used to make up an infant feed. Most bottled water is as safe as the public water supply, but it is certainly no safer. And some is quite definitely unsuitable for infants. Don't use any bottled water whose label includes the words 'natural mineral water' to make up formula – it may contain too many salts and minerals for a baby. All in all, there's no advantage in using bottled water instead of tap water to make up feeds, unless you are on holiday in an area where you know the local water supply is unreliable or unsafe.

Warm bottle in water for a few minutes

GIVING A BOTTLE FEED

How much to give?
Once you have made up the feed accurately, let the baby decide how much to take. It is perfectly all right to put a little more made-up feed into each bottle than is suggested on the packet. Your baby is an individual, not necessarily the formula manufacturer's 'average' baby. His appetite will vary, and he won't be equally hungry at every feed. Trust him to take as much, or as little, as he wants, just as a breast-fed baby can. If you put slightly more than the recom-mended amount for a feed into each bottle, he can take it if he is hungry. But if he loses interest don't try to force him to finish the bottle, even if he has had less than you think he ought to have.

As a very rough guide, most babies need about 170 millilitres or ml (six fluid ounces) of made-up

Test temperature of milk on your wrist

formula for each kilogram of body weight, every 24 hours. A baby who always drains the bottle hungrily at each feed may need rather more than the recommended amount, especially if he cries a lot between feeds. Try adding an extra 50 ml (two fluid ounces) to the bottle at each feed.

Preparing the bottle

Take a bottle from the fridge and turn the teat right way out. Warm the feed by standing the bottle in a bowl of warm water. Never warm a feed in a microwave oven, because although the bottle may feel quite cool to the touch, the milk at the centre of the bottle may be scaldingly hot.

Tilt the bottle when you feed

Check the flow of milk before you start to feed. The hole in the teat should be large enough for two or three drops a second to fall out when the bottle is tilted. Too small a hole will make sucking hard and mean that the baby becomes tired and frustrated. If the hole is too large, the milk will gush out in a continuous stream, making the baby choke and splutter. If the teat isn't right, swap it for another sterile teat and try again, or enlarge the hole with a sterile needle.

Test the temperature by tipping a few drops onto your wrist – it should feel tepid or slightly warm. It is quite safe to give milk at room temperature, or even straight from the fridge, but the baby will probably prefer it warm.

Loosen the cap on the bottle very slightly so that air can enter as the baby sucks milk out.

Giving the bottle

Choose a comfortable chair, with no arms, when you are feeding. Hold your baby cradled with his head supported in the crook of your arm, so that he is feeding in a semi-upright position. It's more difficult for him to swallow if he is lying flat, and he is more likely to choke.

For the first few feeds, you will have to alert the baby's natural sucking reflex in just the same way as a breast-feeding mother does, by gently stroking the cheek nearest to you with a finger or the teat of the bottle.

As the baby turns towards your touch, slip the teat between his lips. He will latch onto it firmly, taking it quite deep into her mouth. Hold the bottle firmly so that the baby can pull against it when he sucks.

Keep the bottle tilted when you are feeding, so that the teat is full of milk. If you hold the bottle horizontally, the teat will be only half full of milk, and the baby will suck in air as well.

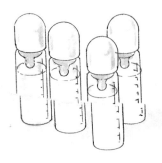
Make several feeds at once

If the teat collapses, pull gently to release the suction and let air flow back into the bottle.

Babies love to suck as well as to feed. So if your baby seems to want to go on sucking even after the bottle is empty, offer the tip of your clean little finger. If he continues to

Types of bottles

suck happily on this, he is not really hungry, just wanting more sucking comfort.

Sometimes a baby will drop off to sleep during a feed, but starts to suck hard whenever you try to take the bottle away. If he won't let go even after a long suck, slip the tip of a finger into his mouth alongside the teat to break the suction.

Winding the baby

Most bottle-fed babies swallow some air when they are feeding, but usually not enough to cause any real discomfort. You can help the baby bring up any wind after a feed (or half-way through if the baby pauses for a rest) by holding him against your shoulder, and rubbing or patting his back gently between the shoulder blades. But if he does not burp within two or three minutes there is no need to go on trying. He probably doesn't need to.

Nearly all babies bring up a little milk when they burp. This is called possetting, and it is quite harmless. However, it's wise to protect your clothes by putting a clean nappy over your shoulder when you wind the baby.

TRAVELLING WITH YOUR BABY

Cartons of ready-made formula (see page 23) are the easiest way to cope with feeds if you are travelling.

But you can take made-up feeds with you. Take them straight from the fridge and put them into an insulated picnic box while they are ice cold, or put them into a plastic bag packed around with chilled, insulated freeze packs. This will keep the feeds at a safe, cool temperature for about eight hours. Carry hot water in a thermos flask and, when you need a feed, warm the bottle by standing it in the hot water. Never carry a warm feed in a thermos. This is a sure way of giving your baby food poisoning.

If you have to travel much with your baby, it is worth buying a wide-topped thermos flask. This can be filled with boiling water, and the bottle put directly in it when a feed needs to be warmed.

CHANGING FROM BREAST-FEEDING TO BOTTLE-FEEDING

If you have started to breast-feed, and want to change to bottle-feeding for any reason, it is best to make the change-over slowly.

Start by offering the baby a bottle at a lunchtime feed. If he won't take it, try again next day at the same feed. Moistening the teat with a few drops of breast milk may encourage the baby to accept a bottle. Once the baby has taken a lunchtime bottle happily for three days, replace a second daytime feed with a bottle, and wait another three days before tackling a third feed. Leave the final bedtime feed until last.

KEY POINTS

✓ Bottle-fed babies, like breast-fed babies, should be demand fed

✓ Take care in choosing a suitable formula

✓ Hygiene and sterilisation of all the equipment used to prepare a feed are very important

✓ Make sure that you use the right kind of water to make up a feed

✓ When travelling never take a warm feed in a thermos – it will give your baby food poisoning

Height and weight gain

Babies born at around the expected time weigh between 2.5 and 4.4 kilograms or kg (5.5–9.75 pounds). The average weight is about 3.5 kg (7 lb 11.5 oz), and the average length 51 centimetres (20 inches).

However, most babies lose about 10 per cent of their birthweight in the first few days. This is normal, and does not mean that the baby isn't getting enough to eat. From about day 5 or 6 the baby will start to gain again, and will probably have regained his birthweight by the time he is 10 days old. After this, a baby's growth is very rapid.

Most babies will have doubled their birthweight by four months and doubled their length by four years. A baby's size at birth is not related to the size he will be as an adult, but, if you keep height and weight charts, after the first year of life you can predict with a fair degree of accuracy what his adult height will be.

In the charts on pages 33–6 the broad coloured band marks the range of measurements likely in normal children. Ninety-four per cent of all children will fall within this range. The darker lines show the average growth curves. Until your baby is over a year, it is easier to check a baby's growth by measuring head circumference (round the largest part of your baby's head, just above the eyebrows and ears) than by measuring length. Each time you measure your baby, mark the measurement on the chart. Join the marks and you will be able to see the pattern of his growth curve. This should follow a steady curve the same shape as the average curve. It may fall either above or below the average curve, but this does not matter. Only if his own curve falls outside the normal range, or if the relative positions of his weight and height curves are very different (for example, if his height falls well below the average

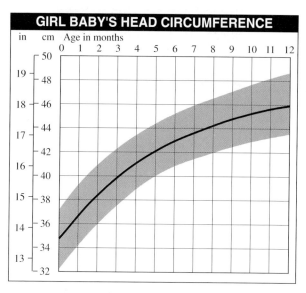

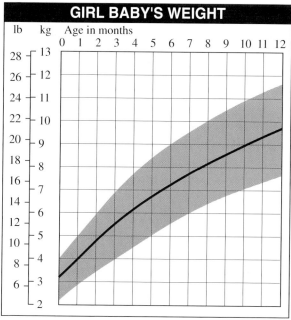

Growth charts for baby girls

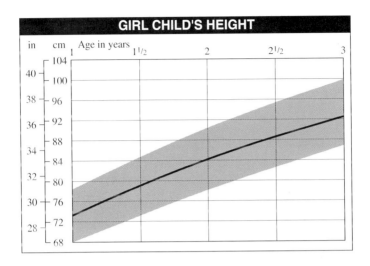

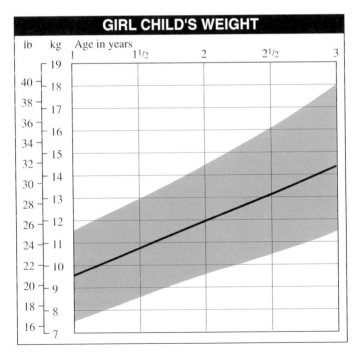

Growth charts for girls aged 1–3

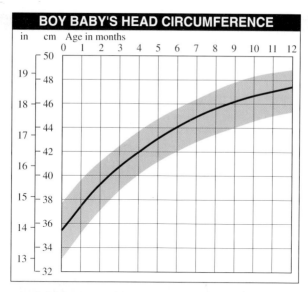

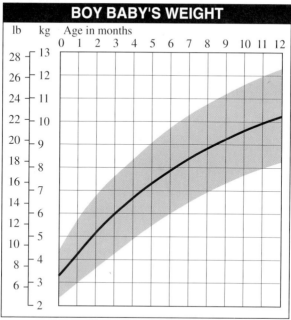

Growth charts for baby boys

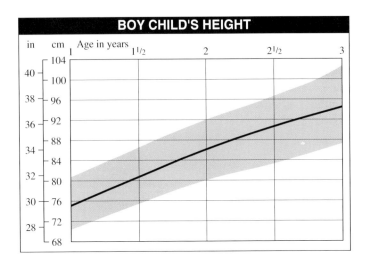

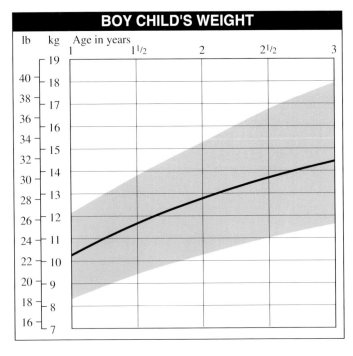

Growth charts for boys aged 1–3

curve and his weight is well above it) need you be concerned about your child's growth. Weight is a less reliable indicator of growth than height – a child who is ill, for example, may lose weight temporarily, although he will soon catch up.

MEASURING YOUR CHILD

During the first year of life your doctor or health visitor will weigh your child regularly and measure the circumference of the baby's head (around the head just above the eyebrows and ears). This is easier to measure than his length, and it is as good a yardstick of growth.

After your child's first birthday, weigh him every six months and, once he can stand, measure his height every six months by standing him against the same patch of wall, feet together and without shoes. Place a ruler on the top of his head, at right angles to the wall to mark his height.

Ask your doctor's advice if your child's weight drops or if any two consecutive measurements are less than you would expect.

KEY POINTS

✓ The average weight of a newborn baby is 3.4 kilograms and the average length 50 centimetres

✓ Ninety-four per cent of all children fall within a certain growth range

Weaning

Very young babies need no other food than milk. But as they grow more active, they need more energy than a milk-only diet can provide, and milk alone no longer gives them all the nutrients that they need. They are also able to bite and chew as well as suck, and you will start to notice that, even after a full feed, your baby still seems hungry. It is no good simply offering more milk – there is a limit to the amount of milk a baby's stomach can hold. So this is the time to start introducing your baby to his first taste of solid food – the process known as weaning.

THE RIGHT TIME TO START WEANING

Weaning a baby takes time. It takes place gradually, over several weeks or even months. And it need not begin at the same age or the same weight for all infants. The length of time that an infant gets everything he needs from breast or formula varies from baby to baby. Babies vary, too, in how quickly and easily they take to the different tastes and textures of a mixed diet. Breast-fed babies gain weight less rapidly from the third month. Boys are bigger than girls, and grow more quickly, so they tend to be given mixed feeding sooner.

It's best not to introduce solid foods too early. Very few infants

First solids

need solid foods before the age of four months, so unless your doctor or health visitor recommends it, it is unwise to start weaning before your baby is four months old. Infants younger than this cannot bite or chew, and they dislike different tastes and textures. Giving energy-rich foods too soon may make them too fat. Even more important, a very young baby is less resistant to infections and more prone to allergy. It is safer to wait till his system is more mature before introducing new items to his diet.

On the other hand, there are disadvantages in leaving weaning too late. It's a good idea to give your baby time to get used to this new way of feeding before he actually needs the food for extra energy, minerals or vitamins. Most babies should be offered a mixed diet not later than the age of six months. By this age your baby will have used up the store of iron he was born with, and will need iron-rich cereals, egg yolk or meat to replenish them. And by delaying too long you may be missing the 'window' during which babies are most willing to try new foods and flavours.

WEANING FROM BREAST OR BOTTLE

The more solid food your baby takes, the less milk she will need. So at the same time as you are introducing her to solid food, you are also gradually weaning her away from the breast or bottle, and getting her used to the idea that drinks can be taken from a cup. This won't happen all at once – even if your baby quite soon shows that she is happy to drink from a cup when she is thirsty, she will probably still want the comfort of sucking from breast or bottle before she goes to bed, and sometimes first thing in the morning too.

Babies usually find it easier to give up the breast than the bottle. A breast-fed baby who is offered milk from a cup at about six months usually takes to it quite quickly, and in a few weeks may be perfectly happy to take all her milk and water from it and not even need a bedtime 'comfort suck'. But a bottle-fed baby may be very reluctant to give up the bottle altogether, especially if you wait till she is older than six months before you introduce her to a cup. Many bottle-fed babies may need a bedtime bottle until they are around a year old.

HOW TO START WEANING

As soon as your baby starts to take solids, at around four months, she will sometimes get thirsty. This is the opportunity you need to introduce her to a cup, rather than offering her a drink in a bottle. It's a good idea to get your baby into the

Next you could try offering a drink of water from a cup instead of a feed if the baby wakes early in the morning. A few weeks later, offer milk from a cup at breakfast too. Don't hurry the process too much, and let the baby finish a feed by sucking if she obviously wants to. Your baby won't take as much milk as she needs from the cup, so it's important not to wean her completely away from breast or bottle too quickly.

If you are breast-feeding, weaning is usually easy. Your breast milk will decrease naturally as the baby takes more from the cup, and the baby will gradually wean herself, though she may continue to want a token bedtime feed from you until nine or ten months. A bottle-fed baby usually still wants a bedtime 'comfort feed' until she is at least a year old.

habit of drinking water when she is thirsty as soon as possible. If you do give fruit juice, make it very dilute and don't offer it more than once a day. Babies quickly get used to sweet, flavoured drinks and may refuse to drink plain water (see page 54).

A few weeks later, at around six months, you can start to offer the baby formula milk from the cup as well. By this age, your baby is probably having three meals a day, consisting of some solid food, topped up by a breast or bottle-feed, as well as a breast or bottle-feed either first thing in the morning or last thing at night, or both. Usually, though, there is one feed a day – usually the lunchtime feed – at which the baby doesn't seem particularly interested in sucking from the breast or bottle; she will probably be quite happy to drink from the cup instead. Give your baby the solids she usually has first, then offer her the cup.

Most babies find a two-handled 'teacher beaker' with spout and lid is the easiest to drink from at first. It

won't be long before the baby tries to grab a handle and hold the cup herself. Let her try to manage alone. Feeling 'I can do it myself' is important to her.

MILK FOR OLDER BABIES

Milk, and milk products, will go on being an important part of your child's diet until she is five years old. Whole, pasteurised milk is suitable for babies aged six months and over, and you can, if you wish, continue to give infant formula. But in both cases your baby will need to be given extra iron and vitamin D – ask your health visitor about this. 'Follow-up' milks – specially prepared for older babies, with extra iron and vitamins added – are suitable too.

Once your baby is over a year, you should give whole cows' milk, which is a good source of energy, protein, calcium and vitamins. Breast milk and infant formula are no longer suitable.

Skimmed and semi-skimmed milks

Many health conscious families nowadays drink skimmed or semi-skimmed milk in preference to whole milk, because they contain less saturated fat. But they also have less vitamin A, and provide less energy, and this makes them unsuitable for babies.

Although whole milk is best for pre-school children, once your child is over two you can gradually introduce semi-skimmed milk into her diet if this is what your family generally uses. Wholly skimmed milk, however, shouldn't be given to any child under the age of five years.

Goats' and sheep's milk are not suitable for infants under six months. These milks can be given to older infants, provided they are pasteurised or boiled. Mineral and vitamin supplements may be needed if these milks are given.

INTRODUCING SOLID FOODS

Most newly weaned infants are quite willing to try most of the foods they are offered, though some are more adventurous than others about trying new tastes or different textures. Older babies are not so adventurous, and most are 'faddy' about certain foods. So take advantage of your infant's early willingness to taste anything, so that she gets used to as wide a range of foods as possible. Once she is familiar with a food she will probably be happy to carry on eating it even when she enters the inevitable 'faddy phase'.

How to feed your baby

To begin with your baby won't want even a taste of whatever solid food you offer unless you let her partially satisfy her hunger by sucking first. It's best to try and 'sandwich' a teaspoonful of cereal or fruit purée between two halves of the normal breast or bottle-feed.

Begin by giving tiny tastes of a food – about enough to cover the tip of a small teaspoon, at just one feed a day. Don't try to cram the spoon into the baby's mouth; just put it gently between her lips and let her suck the food off. If she fusses about taking food from the spoon, try dipping the tip of a clean finger into the food and letting the baby suck that. Once she knows that she likes the taste she won't be so suspicious of the spoon.

Over the next two or three weeks gradually build up the quantity until the baby is taking about two teaspoonfuls. Then start to offer solids at a second feed, again sandwiching them in the middle of the usual breast or bottle. The more your baby eats, the less milk she will need to drink. Soon she should be enjoying her solid food so much that she will be happy to start the meal with it, and just be 'topped up' afterwards with breast or bottle.

Don't worry if your baby clearly dislikes the idea of taking real food when you first try to introduce it. Only a tiny amount of solids is taken at first feeds. If the baby is gaining weight adequately on milk alone, you can delay weaning for a bit longer.

What to give

First foods should be bland, smooth and semi-liquid – in fact as milk-like as possible. Baby rice is a good food to start with, mixed with expressed breast milk, formula or boiled water. When your baby is used to this, try other baby cereals. Next, introduce him to small quantities of cooked and puréed fruits and vegetables.

Puréed apple and baby rice for first foods (the Mouli can be used to purée food)

Try out new foods slowly. Introduce only one new food at a time, and give only a little. If it does seem to disagree with him, you can then avoid it for a few weeks.

At six to eight months introduce puréed meat, chicken and fish, and pieces of banana (which most

Mince or mash chicken, fish or hard-boiled egg for an eight month old

babies love because it is sweet) or apple, cubes of cheese or bread. Remember that a baby can chew very efficiently with his jaws – you need not wait to give hard foods until his teeth have come through.

At about eight months, you can start to mince meat and mash or grate vegetables, rather than puréeing them. A nine-month-old

Chunky textures and plenty of finger foods are good for a nine month old

baby should be able to cope with quite lumpy foods, as well as a variety of finger foods. Don't

broccoli

beans

chicken
chipped

fruit

bread

Finger foods: vegetable sticks, or cheese cut into interesting shapes, makes good finger foods

continue giving smooth purées for too long, or the baby will fuss when introduced to lumpy, textured foods.

FOODS TO AVOID

DON'T GIVE
Whole egg before eight months (egg yolk is fine from six months).
Spinach, turnip and beetroot before six months – they contain a lot of nitrate which can cause problems in young babies.

NEVER GIVE A BABY OR TODDLER PEANUTS
It's easy for a small child to inhale a fragment accidentally, and if this happens the oil the peanuts contain can cause severe irritation in the lungs.

At 10 months your baby should be able to cope with bite-sized pieces of food, and, by a year, he will be able to eat more or less anything the family eats.

Commercial or home made?

Jars of commercial, ready-prepared baby food are usually good value in terms of both nutrition and convenience. The drawback is that the manufacturer's quality control means that they always taste the same.

Try to introduce home-cooked foods too, so that your baby gets used to a wider variety of foods and flavours. Adult convenience and prepackaged foods are not suitable for babies. Many of them may have more sugar, salt or fat than is good for your baby.

Specially prepared commercial baby cereals are better for your baby than ordinary family cereals. They contain vitamins and are fortified with iron. There is no need to add sugar.

Never add salt to your baby's food. Only add the minimum of sugar.

Food preparation tips

If you want to give your baby home-cooked food, use a 'mouli', blender or liquidiser to purée it until the baby is six months old. Peel fruit and vegetables before cooking, and remove pips, or sieve to remove these indigestible parts. If necessary, thin the purée down to a thick cream with milk, water or vegetable stock, or fruit juice, but don't use commercial stock cubes, which have too much added salt.

Learning to feed herself

Your baby will be keen to feed herself long before she's able to do so efficiently. Don't stop your baby 'playing with her food'. Dabbling her fingers in the plate and then licking them may be messy, and make mealtimes long drawn out, but it is worth encouraging. It is her first real step towards independence. If your baby enjoys feeding herself, and finds food interesting and pleasant – not just something that is forced upon her by you – mealtimes are much less likely to be a future problem. Of course she will need your help for a long time yet, but the more practice she gets now, the sooner she will be able to take over completely.

As soon as your baby is able to hold a spoon, at around six months old, give her one and let her use it any way she wants. At first all she will do is wave it around and bite it, but gradually she'll learn to dip it into the food and lick it. By eight months she may even manage to get a partially loaded spoon to her mouth, though it will usually turn over and spill most of its contents on the way. You can help by filling your own spoon and swapping it for her empty one.

By the time she is a year, your baby will be making a reasonable, if messy, attempt at feeding herself. A pre-formed plastic bib with a crumb catcher is the best protection.

Feeding your toddler

Newly weaned infants tend to try most of the foods they are offered. But this period doesn't last long. By the time your child is two she will have developed definite likes and dislikes; she will much prefer familiar foods and be more suspicious about trying new ones. She may even refuse to touch foods that you know perfectly well she has eaten happily in the past.

Food fads

Even if your child is so faddy that there are long periods when she refuses practically everything, she is very unlikely to suffer any serious nutritional deficiency. Don't show that you're upset, or put pressure on her to eat. Just continue to offer a variety of foods, including the things she *will* eat. She won't starve, and curiosity or boredom will eventually persuade her to accept a broader diet. Meanwhile, if your child is full of energy and is growing at the right rate, there is no need to worry about what she eats or how much she eats. (For more detailed information about diet, see

Refusing food

Suspicion of new foods

pages 50–3). It may help to try the following tips.

• **Take advantage of her natural appetite**: at any age, a child is much more likely to be willing to try out a new food, and to accept it, if she is really hungry. So if you want to try out a new dish, choose the mealtime when the child usually has the best appetite.

Make pictures from food

• **Make food look interesting**: you can often make your child more enthusiastic about trying out new foods (or indeed any foods) if you make them look interesting or attractive.

Try arranging a new vegetable with other pieces of food you know that she likes to make a picture on a plate, or to decorate an open sandwich.

• **Try foods in different forms**: if your child doesn't like something, try giving it to her cooked in a different way. If she won't eat cooked vegetables, for example, she might like them raw, or puréed in soup. Egg custard might appeal to a child who won't eat a boiled egg.

- **Have at least some family meals**: children's food preferences are often influenced by what they see others eat. Very young children will tend to prefer things that they see their mothers or other family members choose. Three to four year olds will often try something that they wouldn't otherwise have dreamed of eating if they see their friends enjoying it. So even though it's often more convenient to feed a baby or toddler alone, try to have at least an occasional family meal.

Anger

PREVENTING MEALTIME PROBLEMS

On the whole, children don't have eating problems. It is parents who have the problem – and the problem is usually that their child won't eat what they think she ought to eat, or as much as they think she needs.

It is nearly always a mistake to join battle with a child over feeding. The child invariably wins. There is no way to make a determined child

Feeding himself

Meals should be fun

eat something that she's decided she does not want. And she will be very quick indeed to realise that you really mind what she eats, or whether she eats, or how much she eats, and to take advantage of this. What easier way could there be of gaining your attention, or of asserting her own independence?

The secret of avoiding mealtime problems is to keep the emotional temperature at mealtimes right down. Your aim should be to make your child feel that eating is something she does because he enjoys it, and that meals are meant to be fun for her, and nothing to do with either pleasing you or not pleasing you.

If you are to convince her of this, you have to believe it too, and this isn't as easy as it sounds. It's hard not to be irritated when your child refuses to eat a meal that you've spent money, time and trouble preparing.

Spend a little less time, trouble and money on the meal and you won't mind so much. See it as your job just to provide the food, not to make sure that it's eaten. Leave that up to her.

- Give the child some choice over what to eat and never try to make them eat something they obviously dislike. You won't succeed – in fact you will almost certainly make them dislike it even more.
- Never punish a child for not eating a particular food, and don't reward her for eating something, either. This will only

prove to her how important it is to you.

- Don't try to persuade the child to eat more than she wants. Let her decide when she has had enough. She truly won't starve, even if she doesn't seem to eat as much as you think she should eat.

- Keep meals simple: the more time and trouble a meal have been for you to cook, the more

irritated you will feel if your child refuses to eat it.

- If your child is going through a very faddy phase, stick to familiar foods you know she likes for a while, and don't feel that you are failing as a mother if this means noodles and cheese every night for a week. It may seem monotonous but it will keep the emotional temperature down for both of you.

KEY POINTS

✓ The right time to start weaning a baby is usually between the ages of three and six months

✓ It is often easier to wean a breast-fed baby straight on to a cup than a bottle-fed baby

✓ Don't use semi-skimmed or skimmed milk for a baby and do not give goats' or sheep's milk to infants under six months

✓ First try out different tastes in small quantities – a teaspoon – at one feed in a day

✓ Never give babies whole egg or spinach, turnip and beetroot; never give peanuts to children under five years

Helping your child develop healthy eating habits

Children learn to like what they are given. On the whole they don't need 'special' food – apart from the obvious fact that until they have a full set of teeth their food has to be of a consistency that they can cope with.

There are no foods which are especially 'good' or 'bad' for a child. A child's diet is only unhealthy if he eats too much of some kinds of food, too little of others – or if his total energy intake is so high that he becomes too fat.

Variety is the keynote of a good diet, because all the nutrients that a child needs are present in many different foods. If you introduced your child to a wide variety of foods in his first two years, he would probably eat most things that he's offered quite readily. However, don't be surprised if he starts rejecting things he's often eaten quite happily before (he may be bored with them).

HEALTHY EATING

Most people nowadays know what is meant by a healthy diet. They try to eat less fat and red meat, fewer dairy products and more of the bulky, high-fibre foods which are low in calories, such as cereals, wholemeal bread, fruit and vegetables. For an adult who is hoping to stay healthy and avoid heart disease, this kind of diet is ideal.

However, what is a healthy diet for an adult may not be adequate for a rapidly growing, very active toddler. Small children often eat relatively small quantities of food, for example, so it is important that what they do eat provides them with enough energy.

Children need energy-rich foods such as cheese, eggs, meat and fish. They need full-cream milk, although for adults skimmed or semi-skimmed milk is healthiest (see page 41).

Eating fruit

A diet for all the family

It is perfectly possible to compromise, to give your child a diet that will meet his nutritional and energy needs and yet still help him develop eating habits now which will enable him to stay healthy in adulthood.

Eating is very much a matter of habit: most health-conscious adults have had to make considerable efforts to change their eating habits. With your child you have the chance to form his tastes, so that eating healthily comes naturally to him. If he is never given food that is too sweet or salty, for example, if the butter is always thinly spread on his bread, the chances are that he will grow up to prefer it that way.

If you follow the guidelines in the box on page 52 it will help everyone in the family stay healthy.

Vitamin supplements for older babies and young children

Healthy babies are unlikely to become vitamin deficient. Babies are usually well supplied with vitamins at birth, and for the first six months will get as much as they need from breast milk (if the mother's diet is adequate) or formula. However, after the age of six months babies need extra vitamins, in the form of vitamin drops containing vitamins A, C and D. It's best to give these drops until your baby is at least two years old, and preferably until they are five years old. Babies who were born prematurely may need to be given vitamin drops earlier, from the age of one month.

Snacks and sweets

Toddlers often get hungry between meals – and they are not necessarily hungry at mealtimes. If your child is obviously not hungry for a regular meal, it's best to abandon it and offer the child a snack later on when he may be hungrier.

If the child has missed a meal, don't give sweets or candy bars as a snack. They give the child energy, which he certainly needs, but they don't provide many other nutrients. A cheese or vegetable spread

- Use fresh foods rather than processed foods – they contain more nutrients and usually less fat, salt and sugar. Use only a little salt when you cook and don't add more to food at the table.
- Cut down on red meat (eat it only once or twice a week) and eat more fish and chicken.
- Eat fewer fried foods – grill rather than fry, for example. Spread your butter thinly.
- Use polyunsaturated vegetable oils rather than animal fats for cooking.
- Use wholemeal bread and whole grain cereals.
- Serve vegetables raw if possible, or steam them lightly
- Don't buy sugar-coated cereals, or oversweeten them at the table.
- Don't replace sugar with artificial sweeteners – this simply reinforces everybody's liking for sweet foods. It's much better to get used to foods and drinks that are unsweetened, or at least less heavily sweetened.
- Have fruit or cheese rather than puddings at most meals.

sandwich, with some fruit, makes a healthier snack. However, products containing nuts should not be given to children under one year or, if there is any family history of allergies, to children under seven years.

Cutting down on sugar

All children love sweet things, but sugar can be bad for the teeth. When sugar is allowed to linger in the mouth, acid is formed which attacks the tooth's enamel and leads to dental decay.

Is it sensible to ban sweets altogether? Probably not! You have to be realistic. For the first year or two of your child's life you have more or less complete control over his diet. You can make sure he isn't given any sweets, and limit the amount of sugar in his diet. It makes sense to do this, because it helps to protect his first teeth.

Once your child grows older, and starts to play with other children and visit other homes, there is no way that you will be able to keep him perpetually in a sweet-

Babies need clean teeth when on solid food

free zone. He will still like sweets and sweet foods when he comes across them – and if you have banned them altogether he may covet them even more.

However, the food you provide will certainly influence your child's tastes. There is no need to ban sugar altogether, but if your child is used to a regular diet in which sugar and sugary foods don't play a very prominent part, he won't develop a taste for heavily sweetened foods and it is unlikely he will crave them. You'll not only be safeguarding his teeth, but making it less likely that he will have a weight problem later.

- Give sweets at the end of the meal, and choose ones that can be eaten quite quickly, rather than chewy sticky sweets which have to be sucked for a long time, or that will stick to the teeth.

- Don't give sweets, cakes or biscuits as a between-meals snack – try fruit, cheese or a sandwich instead.

- Don't use sweets as treats or rewards for good behaviour, *or* withhold them as a punishment. This will make them seem very special, and your child will want them even more.

- Make toothbrushing, with a fluoride toothpaste, a routine, after every meal if possible, or at least after breakfast and at bedtime.

- If this isn't possible, try to end the meal with a piece of cheese. This is better than the traditional apple because it helps to neutralise the acid that attacks teeth.

- Never give children a bottle of fruit juice at bedtime so that they suck themselves to sleep.

- If you use a dummy, don't dip it in anything sweet before giving it to the child.

Brushing the teeth can be fun

Children who won't drink water
Plain water seems to have gone out of fashion. One recent study found that over 70% of pre-school children never drink it. Instead they drink fruit juices or squashes. Some drink so much of these sweetened drinks, which contain calories but no real nutrients, that they derive almost a third of their daily energy needs from them. Breakfast may be the only meal at which these children seem really hungry; during the day they eat little and may fail to gain weight.

Children don't need these drinks – there are plenty of other food sources for any vitamins they contain. Try to limit them to a once-a-day treat, and offer water instead when your child is thirsty.

Often, though, a child who has been used to having sweet, flavoured drinks from an early age won't happily settle for water. You may have to 'wean' them, by increasing the intervals between drinks, and gradually making them more dilute.

Vegetarian diet
If you are a vegetarian, you may want to give your child a vegetarian diet too. Provided your diet includes dairy products, its nutritional value will be very similar to that of an ordinary mixed diet. But because it contains a lot of high-fibre foods – fruits, vegetables and cereals – it may not provide enough energy, protein or iron for a small child.

The best sources of iron are red meat, chicken and fish. Although cereals and vegetables also contain iron, it is not absorbed as easily by the body in this form. If you are one of the many vegetarians who also eat fish, your diet will be very healthy indeed. If your child eats neither meat nor fish, it is important for him to have plenty of vitamin C, as this increases the absorption of iron from vegetable sources.

A vegan diet, which contains no animal or dairy foods, must be very carefully planned if it is not to leave a child short of nutrients. Vitamin B_{12}, which is found only in animal foods, will need to be given as a supplement.

If you are in any doubt about whether the diet you prefer is a healthy one for your child, discuss this with your doctor or health visitor.

Fat toddlers

Children grow fat for the same reason that adults grow fat – they eat more than they need, and any excess energy is stored as fat. Common sense will usually tell you if your child is overweight; if he has rolls of fat around his upper arms and thighs, then he probably is too fat.

However, the charts on pages 33–6 will give you a more accurate guide.

HELPING A CHILD SLIM DOWN

- Try to cut down the amount of fat that they eat.
- Dry fry without oil or fat in a non-stick pan.
- Cut the visible fat off meat.
- Use low fat yoghurt and yoghurt-based icecream.
- If your child is over two, give semi-skimmed milk instead of full cream. A child over five can be given fully skimmed milk if he needs to slim down.
- Cut bread more thickly, spread butter more thinly, or use jams or spreads without butter.
- Cut down on fizzy drinks and dilute fruit drinks and squashes well – these all contain a surprising number of calories.
- Offer fewer high-calorie 'extras' such as sweets, crisps or ice creams between meals. The child can still have these as part of his normal meals, but try to get him into the habit of eating fruit or plain bread or biscuits if he needs a snack.
- Encourage more physical play – swimming lessons, visits to a gym, or just a walk to the park every day.

Even if you are worried that your child is too fat, don't try to make him actually lose weight. All that is needed is to gain weight more slowly, so that his height can catch up with his weight. Over a period of several weeks, quite simple adjustments to your child's diet will probably be enough to bring your child's weight gradually within the normal range.

FLUORIDE

Infants and small children need some fluoride (0.25 milligram) each day to make their teeth strong and prevent tooth decay. Neither breast milk nor infant formula contains enough fluoride to meet a baby's needs.

In some parts of the country small amounts of fluoride (only one part per million) are added to the drinking water supply; if you live in one of these and are bottle-feeding, your baby will get enough fluoride from the tap water used to make up his feeds.

But if you are breast-feeding your health visitor will probably advise you to give your baby supplementary fluoride drops. When your baby is older he will get enough fluoride either from tap water or from fluoride tooth-paste; if you carry on giving the drops as well, the baby may get too much fluoride, and this can make the teeth look mottled and unsightly, though it won't actually damage them.

ALLERGY AND INTOLERANCE

Toddlers often dislike certain foods and refuse to eat them. Usually the dislike is only temporary, though it may develop into a real aversion for that food which the child doesn't grow out of for a long time. But this doesn't mean that he has a food allergy.

One of the ways the body protects itself against disease is by making antibodies which counteract harmful invading substances such as bacteria and viruses. In an allergy, antibodies are produced against harmless substances (certain foods, pollens or house dust, for example), and these antibodies cause the release of a chemical, histamine, in the body, which is responsible for a variety of allergic symptoms such as eczema, wheezing and diarrhoea or vomiting.

No-one knows why this happens, although children who have a family history of allergy run a greater than normal risk of developing allergy themselves, but other factors are almost certainly involved as well. Asthma, eczema and hay fever are all symptoms of allergy.

The foods most likely to cause allergic reactions are cows' milk and milk products (by far the most common), eggs (especially the

PRECAUTIONS WHEN THERE IS A FAMILY HISTORY OF ALLERGY

- Breast-feed if you can, because breast-feeding is thought to lessen the risk of a child developing allergies later, or at least to reduce the severity of any allergy that does develop
- If you stop breast-feeding at six months, give infant formula rather than fresh cows' milk. Wait till your baby is a year before introducing cows' milk
- Don't introduce any solid foods before the child is at least three months old
- When you introduce new foods, give only a little to begin with, and introduce only one new food at a time, so that if the child does have a reaction, you know exactly what caused it
- Wait until your child is at least six months before giving eggs, wheat (in bread or cereals) or citrus fruits
- Do not give products containing nuts to your child until he is over seven years

white of the egg), wheat, nuts and citrus fruits. If you think your child reacts badly to a particular food, withdraw it for a few days and see if the symptoms disappear, but talk to your doctor before you make any major or prolonged changes in a child's diet. Soya-based milks can be used for infants who cannot tolerate cows' milk, provided you use a specially prepared infant formula.

Although it is important always to seek a dietician's advice before restricting your child's diet in any significant way, if there is a strong history of allergy in either your family or your partner's, it is worth taking some precautions.

Food intolerance

A few infants and children have digestive disorders which mean that they cannot digest or absorb some components of their diet. A few babies, for example, lack the enzyme (lactase) which digests the sugar in milk. The undigested sugar ferments in the bowel, causing frothy, explosive diarrhoea.

In a small number of children, gluten (a protein found in wheat, rye and certain other cereals) damages the intestinal wall so that it cannot absorb many important nutrients. Symptoms appear within six months of introducing gluten into a baby's diet – the baby loses weight and has bulky, pale, greasy-looking and offensive smelling stools.

Such children all need special diets, supervised by a dietician, to exclude these particular foods from their diet.

KEY POINTS

✓ Variety is the key of a good diet

✓ Children need energy-rich foods

✓ Give cheese or fruit or a vegetable spread sandwich as a snack, not sweets

✓ Encourage your child to drink water

✓ If there is a family history of allergy in your or your partner's family, then precautions should be taken with your child's feeding

Index